Knoppix
Pocket Reference

Knoppix
Pocket Reference

Kyle Rankin

Beijing · Cambridge · Farnham · Köln · Paris · Sebastopol · Taipei · Tokyo

Knoppix Pocket Reference
by Kyle Rankin

Copyright © 2005 O'Reilly Media, Inc. All rights reserved.
Printed in the United States of America.

Published by O'Reilly Media, Inc., 1005 Gravenstein Highway North,
Sebastopol, CA 95472.

O'Reilly books may be purchased for educational, business, or sales
promotional use. Online editions are also available for most titles
(*safari.oreilly.com*). For more information, contact our corporate/
institutional sales department: (800) 998-9938 or *corporate@oreilly.com*.

Editor:	David Brickner
Production Editor:	Claire Cloutier
Cover Designer:	Emma Colby
Interior Designer:	David Futato

Printing History:

June 2005:	First Edition.

0-596-10075-2
[C]

Contents

Knoppix Pocket Reference

Introduction

Knoppix is a complete Linux distribution, created by Klaus Knopper, that runs from a bootable CD-ROM. A Knoppix CD contains over 2 GB of files in its compressed filesystem, including a complete desktop environment, web browsers, an office suite, network tools, and even games. Knoppix requires no installation to use, and when it shuts down, it leaves the underlying system in its previous state.

This book's purpose is to pack all of the information you might need when using Knoppix into a format you can easily carry around with you. Knoppix fits enormous functionality into a pocket size, so why shouldn't its reference do the same? System administrators and power users of Linux and Windows alike will find ready access to the rescue instructions they need when the worst has happened to their system. Knoppix fans will find cheat codes (options passed to Knoppix at boot time) organized into categories and common Knoppix functions documented and easy to locate. Knoppix experts interested in remastering (creating your own live distribution—see the later section "Remaster Knoppix") can quickly determine the function of important files, along with each of the shell commands that make remastering possible.

The official web site for Knoppix is *http://www.knoppix.org*; it contains information about the project, including some documentation and a list of mirror sites for the 700MB CD-ROM install image. After you download the ISO image, write it to a CD using your CD writing software's Burn Image option. Knoppix CD-ROMs are also available from a number of web retailers that sell other Linux distribution CD-ROMs—a list of retailers is available on the Knoppix site.

Knoppix has a vibrant community. The web site *http://www.knoppix.net* hosts a large English-speaking forum for answering questions, and also contains a number of HOW-TOs and other documentation for the Knoppix project.

This pocket reference is current to Knoppix Version 3.7. For the most part, methods and cheat codes are applicable across current and future versions of Knoppix, but Knoppix is a continually evolving project with new features added all the time. Even as this book is being written, Knoppix 3.8—with its UnionFS system—promises some totally new opportunities for Knoppix data persistence (more on that in the later "Experimental Features" section).

Conventions Used in This Book

The following is a list of the typographical conventions used in this book:

Italic

> Used to indicate URLs and email addresses, command or program names, filenames, filename extensions, and directory/folder names. Also used to introduce or emphasize terms. For example, a path in the filesystem will appear as */Developer/Applications*.

`Constant width`

> Used to show code examples, the contents of files, and console output, as well as command options and the names of variables.

Constant width bold
> Used to display commands or text that the user should type directly.

Constant width italic and ***constant width bold italic***
> Used in tables and man page listings (and command examples, respectively) to show sample text to be replaced with your own values.

You should pay special attention to notes set apart from the text with the following styles:

TIP

This is a tip, suggestion, or general note. It contains useful supplementary information about the topic at hand.

WARNING

This is a warning or note of caution.

How to Contact Us

We have tested and verified the information in this book to the best of our ability, but you may find that features have changed (or even that we have made mistakes!).

As a reader of this book, you can help us to improve future editions by sending us your feedback. Please let us know about any errors, inaccuracies, bugs, misleading or confusing statements, and typos that you find anywhere in this book.

Please also let us know what we can do to make this book more useful to you. We take your comments seriously and will try to incorporate reasonable suggestions into future editions. You can write to us at:

O'Reilly Media, Inc.
1005 Gravenstein Hwy N.
Sebastopol, CA 95472
(800) 998-9938 (in the U.S. or Canada)
(707) 829-0515 (international/local)
(707) 829-0104 (fax)

To ask technical questions or to comment on the book, send email to:

bookquestions@oreilly.com

The web site for the *Knoppix Pocket Reference* lists examples, errata, and plans for future editions. You can find this page at:

http://www.oreilly.com/catalog/knoppixpr

For more information about this book and others, see the O'Reilly web site:

http://www.oreilly.com

Cheat Codes

Cheat codes are options, passed to Knoppix at boot time, that can change many of Knoppix's settings. Cheat codes have this format:

```
boot: kernel option1 option2 ...
```

The first argument is always the kernel to boot from (knoppix by default), followed by any number of other options. For example, to tell Knoppix to check the CD for errors, at the boot: prompt you would type:

```
knoppix testcd
```

To see a list of commonly used cheat codes, press F2 or F3 at the boot: prompt or read the *knoppix-cheatcodes.txt* file in the *KNOPPIX* directory on the CD. If no cheat codes are entered, Knoppix will continue the boot process with defaults. Table 1 lists the basic cheat codes used with Knoppix.

Table 1. Basic cheat codes

Cheat code	Description
testcd	Check CD data integrity and MD5sums.
2	Runlevel 2, text mode.
noeject	Don't eject CD after halt.
noprompt	Don't prompt to remove the CD at shutdown.
splash	Boot with a fancy animated splash screen.
lang=cn|de|da|es|fr|it|nl|pl|ru|sk|tr|tw|us	Specify system language/keyboard.
keyboard=*us*	Use different console keyboard.
xkeyboard=*us*	Use a different X keyboard.
gmt	Set time zone to GMT.
tz=America/New_York	Use specified time zone.
blind	Start Braille terminal (no X).
brltty=type,port,table	Parameters for Braille devices.

Kernel Modes

Since Version 3.4, Knoppix has included both the 2.4 and 2.6 series kernels. It also allows you to use special kernel modes (essentially kernels with extra arguments) at the boot: prompt.

Kernel modes differ from cheat codes in that you may choose only one kernel mode at the boot: prompt, and it must be the first argument that you type. Table 2 provides a list of kernel choices.

Table 2. Kernel choices

Kernel	Description
knoppix	Default Knoppix kernel.
knoppix24	Use 2.4 kernel.
knoppix26	Use 2.6 kernel.
expert	Boot into expert mode.
expert26	Expert mode with 2.6 kernel.
failsafe	Boot with almost no hardware detection.
fb1280x1024	Use 1280×1024 fixed framebuffer.
fb1024x768	Use 1024×768 fixed framebuffer.
fb800x600	Use 800×600 fixed framebuffer.
memtest	Rum Memtest86+ instead of Linux.

TIP

Knoppix 3.8 and later contain only the 2.6 kernel, so 2.4 kernel options are deprecated in those versions.

Check RAM for Errors with Memtest86+

Memtest86+ is a standalone, BIOS-based memory test designed for x86 computers. It's an updated version of the original Memtest86 software that adds more updated hardware compatibility. The official project page is at *http://www.memtest.org* and lists detailed information about the program.

This software is included with Knoppix and can be launched with the memtest kernel mode option. Instead of booting into Knoppix, you boot directly into the Memtest86+ software and start the scan. Memtest86+ runs a number of types of memory tests in an indefinite loop, but a single pass should be sufficient to determine whether a system has bad memory that should be replaced. RAM errors can lead to frustrating system instability and random lockups. Memtest86+ runs several relatively quick tests that include writing different patterns of data to RAM, checking to see whether the areas that were written to report the correct information, and checking that neighboring blocks of RAM weren't influenced by what was written. Even if you have bad RAM, you might pass many—if not most—of the tests that Memtest86+ performs, so by default Knoppix has Memtest86+ run all of its tests, each designed to highlight different potential RAM problems.

As Memtest86+ runs, it reports any errors it finds at each phase of the test directly on the screen, along with a running tally. You also have the option of outputting a BadRAM pattern instead. BadRAM is a Linux kernel patch created by Rick van Rein and hosted at *http://rick.vanrein.org/linux/*. This patch allows you to tell the Linux kernel to ignore bad sections of memory, so that it can continue with what is left. By doing this, you don't necessarily have to throw away RAM that has errors. To tell Memtest86+ to output BadRAM patterns, type **c** to pause the test and enter the configuration menu, **6** to enter Error Report Mode, and **2** to select BadRAM patterns. Then hit **8** to restart the test.

TIP

By default, Memtest86+ will launch directly into the test, but if you are an advanced user, you can press **c** to enter the configuration menu and change test settings.

If you are interested in what Memtest86+ is doing (on a basic level), here are the different test descriptions from the Memtest86+ documentation:

Test 0 (Address test, walking ones, no cache)
Tests all address bits in all memory banks by using a "walking ones" address pattern. A *walking pattern* initializes the RAM to zero, then writes a one (or other pattern) to a location and reads all other locations to make sure that they are still zero. Then it verifies the first location, reinitializes all the RAM to zero, and repeats the pattern at the next location until all the RAM has been tested.

Test 1 (Address test, own address)

Each address is written with its own address and then is checked for consistency. In theory, previous tests should have caught any memory addressing problems. This test should catch any addressing errors that somehow were not previously detected.

Test 2 (Moving inversions, ones and zeros)

This test uses the moving inversions algorithm, which shifts the data pattern left one bit for each successive address, with patterns of all ones and zeros. Caching is enabled, even though it interferes to some degree with the test algorithm. With the cache enabled, this test does not take long and should quickly find all "hard" errors (errors that always occur) and some more subtle errors. This test is only a quick check.

Test 3 (Moving inversions, eight bit pat)

This test is the same as test 1, but uses an 8-bit-wide pattern of walking ones and zeros. This test will better detect subtle errors in "wide" memory chips (chips that store data more than one bit wide). A total of 20 data patterns are used.

Test 4 (Moving inversions, random pattern)

Test 4 uses the same algorithm as test 1, but the data pattern is a random number and its binary complement. This test is particularly effective in finding difficult-to-detect errors that vary depending on what data is written to RAM. A total of 60 patterns are used. The random number sequence is different with each pass, so multiple passes increase effectiveness.

Test 5 (Block move, 64 moves)

This test stresses memory by using block move (movsl) instructions, and is based on Robert Redelmeier's burnBX test. Memory is initialized with shifting patterns that are inverted every 8 bytes. Then 4MB blocks of memory are moved around using the movsl instruction.

After the moves are completed, the data patterns are checked. Because the data is checked only after the memory moves are completed, it is not possible to know where the error occurred. The addresses reported are only where the bad pattern was found. Because the moves are constrained to an 8MB segment of memory, the failing address will always be less than 8 MB away from the reported address. Errors from this test are not used to calculate BadRAM patterns.

Test 6 (Moving inversions, 32-bit pattern)

This test is a variation of the moving inversions algorithm. The starting bit position is shifted left for each pass. To use all possible data patterns, 32 passes are required. This test is quite effective at detecting data sensitive errors, but the execution time is long.

Test 7 (Random number sequence)

This test writes a series of random numbers into memory. By resetting the seed for the random number, the same sequence of numbers can be created for a reference. The initial pattern is checked and then complemented and checked again on the next pass. However, unlike with the moving inversions test, writing and checking can be done only in the forward direction.

Test 8 (Modulo 20, ones and zeros)

Using the Modulo-X algorithm should uncover errors that are not detected by moving inversions due to cache and buffering interference with the algorithm. As with test 1, only ones and zeros are used for data patterns.

Test 9 (Bit fade test, ninety minutes, two patterns)

The bit fade test initializes all of memory with a pattern and then sleeps for 90 minutes. Then memory is examined to see whether any memory bits have changed. All ones and all zero patterns are used. This test takes three hours to complete. The bit fade test is not included in the normal test sequence and must be run manually via the runtime configuration menu.

As the test runs, you can keep track of which test phase is currently running, how many errors have been detected, which test phase caused the errors, and how many passes have been performed. The test will cycle indefinitely; one or two passes are generally enough to identify any major problems with your RAM. When you are satisfied with the number of passes, hit Esc to exit. If you have errors, there are a number of ways to proceed. If you have multiple memory modules, you can try removing all but one at a time, so that you can isolate which one is problematic. Sometimes memory causes errors only on a particular machine, so move the module to a new machine and run Memtest86+ on the new machine.

TIP

There have been a number of reports of errors for tests 5 and 8 on Athlon systems, even with name-brand memory and a quality motherboard. The creator of Memtest86+ insists that these errors are legitimate and that even if the RAM isn't necessarily bad, it still does not seem able to run at Athlon speeds. His suggested remedy is to either choose more conservative memory timings on the motherboard, or replace the memory with higher-quality memory that can sustain those speeds.

X Settings

You can use cheat codes to change many of the X settings from what Knoppix detects to something more suitable for your hardware. For instance, Knoppix might choose a screen resolution that's too high for your taste, so you could specify a lower resolution with the following command at the boot: prompt:

```
knoppix screen=800x600
```

Knoppix defaults to the X Version 4 server. If you have a particularly old video card, X Version 4 might not support it well, so Knoppix still includes X Version 3. You can use these modules instead with the xserver cheat code. To use the XF86_Mach64 module for certain ATI cards, type this at the boot: prompt:

```
knoppix xserver=XF86_Mach64
```

Table 3 lists the cheat codes that allow you to tweak X settings.

Table 3. X cheat codes

Cheat code	Description
desktop=fluxbox| icewm|kde|larswm| twm|wmaker|xfce	Use specified window manager.
screen=*1280x1024*	Use specified screen resolution for X.
depth=*16*	Use specified color depth.
xvrefresh=60 (or vsync=60)	Use 60kHz vertical refresh rate.
xhrefresh=80 (or hsync=80)	Use 80kHz horizontal refresh rate.
nowheelmouse	Force plain PS/2 protocol for PS/2 mouse.
xmodule=ati|fbdev| mga|nv|radeon|savage| s3|svga|i810|vesa	Use specified X Version 4 module.
xserver=Xfree86| XF86_3Dlabs|XF86_8514| XF86_AGX|XF86_I128| XF86_Mach32|XF86_Mach64| XF86_P9000|XF86_S3| XF86_S3V|SF86_SVGA| XF86_VGA16|XF86_W32	Use specified X Version 3 server.

Kiosk Mode

Knoppix 3.6 and later versions implement a native kiosk mode that allows a user to start a basic desktop that launches only a web browser that defaults to a predetermined HTML file. This HTML file employs JavaScript to start a special kiosk-mode browser window, open to any URL you choose. To enable kiosk mode, use the desktop cheat code as though you were setting a window manager, but specify **kiosk** as your window manager. A second cheat code, url, lets you specify the URL the kiosk will automatically open. You can point this kiosk to a file on the local system, or a URL somewhere on the Internet or corporate intranet.

For instance, to boot Knoppix into kiosk mode and load the main O'Reilly page, type this at the boot: prompt:

```
knoppix desktop=kiosk url=http://www.oreilly.com
```

Hardware Codes

Knoppix's hardware detection is good, but it isn't always perfect. Luckily, you can use cheat codes to change many of the hardware settings and enable or disable detection for certain types of hardware.

You can also take advantage of normal Linux kernel arguments such as you might use with *lilo* or *grub* to change options that you pass to the kernel. Many of these options may be necessary in order to boot on difficult hardware, such as a laptop. Table 4 lists the hardware cheat codes that Knoppix offers.

Table 4. Hardware cheat codes

Cheat code	Description
dma	Enable DMA for all IDE drives.
nodma	Disable DMA for all IDE drives. Particularly useful if you are getting read errors on your CD-ROM.
alsa	Use ALSA sound drivers (autodetect).
alsa=es1938	Use specified ALSA module.
noswap	Don't attempt to mount any detected swap drives. This code is particularly useful for computer forensics.

Table 4. Hardware cheat codes (continued)

Cheat code	Description
atapicd	Don't use SCSI emulation for IDE CD-ROMs.
usb2	Try to initialize USB 2.x controllers; otherwise, controllers will use USB 1.1.
noapm	Disable Advanced Power Management.
noaudio	Disable all audio.
nofirewire	Disable all FireWire ports.
nopcmcia	Disable PCMCIA slot.
noscsi	Disable all SCSI devices.
nousb	Disable all USB ports.

Like any other Linux distribution, Knoppix can also use standard kernel arguments to tweak how and whether the kernel accesses certain hardware. Table 5 lists some common kernel arguments that you can use to configure the kernel on Knoppix—or any other Linux distribution.

Table 5. Common kernel arguments

Kernel option	Description
mem=*128M*	Specify memory size in kilobytes (K), megabytes (M), or gigabytes (G).
pnpbios=off	Disable PnP BIOS initialization.
acpi=off	Disable ACPI (Advanced Configuration and Power Interface) power management. Many problems with booting Linux on a machine (particularly a laptop) can be fixed by disabling ACPI.
acpi=force	Enable ACPI if default was off.
acpi=noirq	Don't use ACPI for IRQ routing.
pci=bios	Workaround for bad PCI controllers.
ide2=0x180 nopcmcia	Boot from PCMCIA CD-ROM (some notebooks).
pci=irqmask=0x0e98	Try this code if your PS/2 mouse doesn't work.

Table 5. Common kernel arguments (continued)

Kernel option	Description
noapic	Disable APIC (Advanced Programmable Interrupt Controller) on the system. APIC is sometimes the cause of lockups at boot. Try disabling it to get further in the boot process.
noagp	Disable hardware detection on the AGP slot.
noapm	Disable Advanced Power Management.
noaudio	Disable all audio.
nofirewire	Disable all FireWire ports.
nopcmcia	Disable PCMCIA slot.
noscsi	Disable all SCSI devices.
nosmp	Use a single processor on SMP systems.
nousb	Disable all USB ports.

Framebuffer Support

You can also take advantage of framebuffer support in the kernel to create a console with a specific color depth and resolution. Pass the arguments in Table 6 to the vga= option to set the framebuffer console. For instance, to create a 1024×768 console with 64,000 colors, use this command:

```
knoppix vga=791
```

To disable framebuffer support altogether and provide the standard 25×80 VGA console, use this command:

```
knoppix vga=normal
```

If you want a console-only environment without X, use the 2 cheat code:

```
knoppix 2
```

Table 6. Linux kernel framebuffer arguments

Colors	640×480	800×600	1024×768	1280×1024
256	769	771	773	775
32k	784	787	790	793
64k	785	788	791	794
16M	786	789	792	795

Free Up the CD-ROM

While Knoppix is relatively responsive when compared with other live CDs, running directly from a CD-ROM can be rather slow. Knoppix has a number of options that allow you to use a copy of the CD from either RAM or a hard drive; this not only speeds up the system considerably, but also frees up the CD-ROM drive for other uses. Table 7 lists the cheat codes that make this possible.

Table 7. Cheat codes that free up the CD-ROM

Cheat code	Description
toram	Copy CD to RAM and run from there.
tohd=*/dev/hda1*	Copy CD to specified partition and run from there.
fromhd	Skip checking for Knoppix on CD-ROM.
fromhd=*/dev/hda1*	Boot from previously copied CD on specified partition.
bootfrom=*/dev/hda1*	Boot from previously copied CD image on specified partition.
bootfrom=*/dev/hda1/KNX.iso*	Boot from specified CD image.
knoppix_dir=*KNOPPIX*	Directory to search for on the CD (defaults to *KNOPPIX*).
knoppix_name=*KNOPPIX*	The name of the compressed loopback filesystem to use on the CD.

If you have at least a gigabyte of RAM, the toram cheat code provides the fastest Knoppix environment, because the entire CD is copied and then run from RAM.

There are a number of options to consider if you plan on running Knoppix from a hard drive. The tohd cheat code copies the entire CD to a directory on the specified partition and boots from it, while fromhd boots from a previously copied directory.

The bootfrom cheat code can boot from a CD image (an actual *iso*) on the system, provided that its kernel and the kernel on the CD are the same. This method is particularly useful if you are remastering Knoppix (see "Remaster Knoppix" later in the book) and want to try out your changes before burning it to a CD. Here is an example of the bootfrom cheat code, using wildcards in the argument:

```
knoppix bootfrom=/dev/hda1/K*.iso
```

This command would use a *Knoppix.iso* image on the */dev/hda1* partition, provided it is the only file in that directory that begins with *K* and ends with *.iso*.

The knoppix_dir and knoppix_name cheat codes are useful if you need to rename a *KNOPPIX* directory (as is the case with the tohd cheat code) or the *KNOPPIX* compressed image file you have stored on a hard drive, as these cheat codes let you specify an alternative name for that directory and filesystem, respectively.

These codes can also be useful for remastering, because they allow you to maintain multiple *KNOPPIX* directories and *KNOPPIX* cloop (compressed loopback) filesystems on a hard drive and choose between them at boot. You could even put multiple Knoppix variants on a single DVD and use this cheat code to choose between them.

Special Knoppix Tools

For the most part, all of the tools and programs available on a Knoppix CD are also available on other Linux distributions. However, there are a few tools created specifically for Knoppix. The majority of these tools are collected in the K → KNOPPIX menu and are organized into the following general categories of use:

Configure
> Here you will find a number of wizards to help automate the process of setting up hardware such as TV cards, printers, and sound cards. Tools for persistent settings across reboots are also here.

Network/Internet
> So many wizards exist for setting up different kinds of network connections that it justifies its own category under the KNOPPIX menu. Go here for help when your network isn't automatically configured.

Services
> Knoppix includes a number of servers, such as *ssh*, *NX*, *syslog*, Samba, and terminal servers. You can configure and start these services easily from scripts in this menu.

Utilities
> This category houses various utilities to aid in using your Knoppix environment. The Captive NTFS wizard (necessary for mounting NTFS partitions read/write), boot floppy creation script, live software installer, and other utilities fall under this menu.

Root Shell
> Not really a category on its own; this option gives you an xterm with root privileges.

The following sections will introduce you to these Knoppix-specific tools.

Persistent Settings

Even though Knoppix runs from a read-only CD-ROM, it includes the *saveconfig* and *mkpersistenthome* scripts to save and maintain different types of settings and other data across reboots. Without this feature, any changes you might make to your desktop and any files you create would be deleted once you reboot. With these scripts, you can take your Knoppix CD with you to multiple computers, and your files and settings will follow you.

saveconfig

The *saveconfig* script allows you to save your personal settings, the *~/Desktop* directory, network settings, graphics settings, and other system configuration settings. To launch the script, either type **saveconfig** in a terminal or click K → KNOPPIX → Configure → "Save Knoppix configuration." Specify which settings to save from the list that appears, and then which device on the system to save to, including USB drives, floppies, and hard drives. The script then creates *configs.tbz* and *knoppix.sh* files on the selected media. The first is a tarball of all the files you saved; the second is a script that Knoppix will run to extract the files when you choose one of the cheat codes from Table 8.

Table 8. Persistent settings

Cheat code	Description
floppyconfig	Run *knoppix.sh* from a floppy.
myconf=/dev/sda1	Run *knoppix.sh* from specified partition.
myconf=/dev/sda1/dir	Run *knoppix.sh* from specified directory.
myconf=scan	Scan the system for *knoppix.sh*.

By default, any *knoppix.sh* scripts that are found are not automatically executed, with one exception. If you place a *knoppix.sh* script inside the *KNOPPIX* directory on the CD, Knoppix will automatically execute that script each time you boot, without requiring that any cheat codes be used.

Any changes you make to settings after you run *saveconfig* require that you run *saveconfig* again.

Customize what you back up

Since *configs.tbz* is just a tar archive compressed with *bzip2*, you can bypass the normal *saveconfig* script altogether and instead create the archive yourself from the command line. Doing this enables you to specify exactly what you want to back up. For example, the following command backs up your Mozilla and Netscape settings:

```
$ BZIP2=-9 tar -cpPjf configs.tbz \
/home/knoppix/.mozilla /home/knoppix/.netscape
```

You can add any number of files and directories to this list, provided that they are writable (that is, on the ramdisk). Candidates include files in */etc*, all of */home*, */tmp*, and */var*.

You can even modify a *configs.tbz* file after the fact to update, add, or delete files. This trick provides a quick shortcut to recreating the entire file, as you can add, remove, or update individual files or directories. You might use this method if you are mostly pleased with the files that *saveconfig* backs up and want to add only one extra directory. First decompress the tar file, with:

```
$ bunzip2 configs.tbz
```

To add a file, replace the c argument (create) with the r argument (append):

```
$ tar -rpPf configs.tar /path/to/file
```

To delete a file, replace the c argument with the --delete argument:

```
$ tar --delete -pPf configs.tar /path/to/file
```

When you are happy with your changes, compress the tar file and rename it to its original name:

```
$ BZIP2=-9 bzip2 configs.tar
$ mv configs.tar.bz2 configs.tbz
```

TIP

You can even maintain multiple *configs.tbz* files, each in its own directory. To point Knoppix to the correct file, just add the directory to the end of the myconf path.

Persistent home directory

If you plan on using Knoppix as a portable Linux distribution, you might want to save your entire home directory so that it can be restored at each boot. Type mkpersistenthome in a terminal or click K → KNOPPIX → Configure → "Create a persistent KNOPPIX home directory" to launch a script that makes this process very easy.

You can specify whether this script should use an entire partition or create a loopback file for the home directory on any writable device that Knoppix detects. If you choose an entire partition, Knoppix will format and copy the home directory there. If you choose a loopback file, Knoppix will create a *knoppix.img* loopback file on the media you chose.

To use the persistent home directory, use the cheat codes from Table 9. Unlike the *saveconfig* script, any changes made to a persistent home directory will persist across reboots without rerunning the script.

Table 9. Persistent home cheat codes

Cheat code	Description
home=*/dev/sda1/knoppix.img*	Mount loopback file as */home/knoppix*.
home=scan	Scan the system for a Knoppix home directory.

Window Manager Memory Requirements

One downside to a distribution that runs completely from CD is that it needs a lot of RAM to run at best performance. Different desktop environments on the CD require that you have a certain amount of RAM before they will load. Table 10 lists the minimum free RAM requirements for desktop environments under Knoppix. (Note that not all desktop environments listed are on the Knoppix CD, though they may be found on Knoppix variants.) If a machine does not have enough free RAM for the chosen desktop environment, Knoppix will use the TWM window manager instead.

Table 10. Desktop environment memory requirements

Desktop environment	Minimum free RAM (bytes)
KDE	60,000
GNOME	45,000
Larswm	35,000
Enlightenment	35,000
Fluxbox	35,000
XFCE3	35,000
XFCE4	35,000
Windowmaker	35,000
IceWM	35,000

Swap File Configuration

Knoppix will automatically use any swap partitions it finds on the system by default. If you need more memory under Knoppix, you can create a swap file on a *natively writable* Windows partition (FAT or FAT32). Select K → KNOPPIX → Configure → "SWAP file configuration" for a wizard to automate the process.

Network Configuration

Under the Network/Internet menu, you will find scripts to automate the configuration of many different kinds of network connections. By default, Knoppix will attempt to detect any Ethernet or wireless cards on the system and will obtain an IP address via DHCP. If your hardware isn't supported, or your network requires some extra configuration, the tools described here will help automate the process:

/dev/modem Connection Setup
> If you use a modem to connect to the Internet, use this script to configure what hardware the */dev/modem* device points to. You can choose from a number of different modem devices, including serial, USB, IrDA, Bluetooth, and even a winmodem, if Knoppix supports it.

ADSL/PPPOE Configuration
> If you have a DSL connection that requires you to connect each time with a login and password, chances are that you have a PPPoE (Point-to-Point Protocol over Ethernet) connection. This script checks whether your network uses PPPoE, and if so, prompts you for the username and password to connect to the network.

GPRS Connection
> This script automates the process of connecting to a GPRS Internet connection over a cell phone. If you have not yet run the */dev/modem* Connection Setup script, it will launch, so that you can choose how you will connect to the cell phone. Then you will be able to choose your GPRS provider and connect to the network.

ISDN Connection
> Fairly self-explanatory; this script automates the process of configuring an ISDN connection under Knoppix.

Modem Dialer
> Once you configure your modem with the */dev/modem* Connection Setup script, run this script to actually dial and connect to your ISP.

Network Card Configuration

If your network uses static IP addresses, or if for some other reason Knoppix was unable to get your Ethernet card on the network correctly, run this script and enter your network settings manually.

Wavelan Configuration

If you use a wireless card and need to enter special network settings (such as WEP keys), run this script to configure and connect to your wireless network.

Ndiswrapper Configuration

There are a number of wireless cards that are not yet natively supported by Linux. Even so, many of these cards can work with the appropriate Windows driver and *ndiswrapper*. This script automates the process of setting up *ndiswrapper* with your wireless card and requires that you have the *.dll* files for your driver under Windows (either extracted from a setup program beforehand, or found on the Windows partition on the system).

Knoppix Terminal Server

The Knoppix Terminal Server script sets up everything that you need to boot any other netboot-capable machine (PXE or Etherboot) on the network from a single Knoppix CD. The client machines access the programs from the NFS-mounted Knoppix CD, but will still be using their CPU and RAM to run applications.

First, make sure that your network card is configured properly and is functioning on the network; then select K → KNOPPIX → Services → Start KNOPPIX Terminal Server. Choose Setup from the list of options. When the wizard prompts you for network drivers to probe for, be sure that all the network drivers your client machines need are checked. Next, choose from among a number of extra terminal server options, which are listed in Table 11. You can then enter any cheat codes you want to automatically enable on client machines.

Table 11. Terminal server options

Option	Description
Secure	Disable root access on all clients.
Masq	IP masquerading and forwarding.
DNS	Set up a nameserver cache and proxy.
Squid	Enable a transparent web proxy.
NX	NX thin client setup.

WARNING

The terminal server script will set up and start its own DHCP server, so be sure that any other DHCP servers on the same network are disabled, so that they don't conflict.

Once the terminal server is set up, you are dropped back to the first menu. Choose Start; the terminal server will start in the background. To connect to the terminal server, boot any netbootable machine and make sure to choose the netboot option in your BIOS. To stop the terminal server, rerun the script and choose Stop from the initial list of options.

Samba Server

Knoppix includes Samba, so that you can easily share files on the Knoppix filesystem, or on partitions underneath, to Windows desktops or other SMB-capable computers. If you are comfortable with Samba configuration, you can just edit */etc/samba/smb.conf* directly and then start the service by running this command in a terminal:

```
$ sudo /etc/init.d/samba start
```

Otherwise, click K → KNOPPIX → Services → Start Samba Server. This will wipe out any previous Samba configuration it finds (the default Knoppix configuration, or even a configuration file that you created by hand), and allow you to share all of the hard drives on the system or just your home directory and any printers you have configured.

If you used the wizard, you can go back and edit the /etc/samba/smb.conf file afterward to tweak settings and then restart the server with this command:

```
$ sudo /etc/init.d/samba restart
```

Live Software Installer

Knoppix includes a lot of software, but for whatever reason—whether because of space constraints, licensing issues, or other reasons—it can't include everything. Because the CD is read-only, you can't just install software to the /usr directory. The live software installer remedies these problems by providing a method to download and install certain programs to the home directory.

TIP

With the new UnionFS system, Knoppix no longer needs to use the live software installer. Check out the later "Experimental Features" section for more details.

Click K → KNOPPIX → Utilities → "Install Software while running from CD" or launch the live installer with this command:

```
$ knx-live-inst.sh
```

This brings up an interface that lets you choose what software to install. After you've made your selections, the program downloads and installs the software into the ~/.dist directory.

Because these programs are installed into ramdisk, they
will be deleted when you reboot. While each program is
relatively small, be sure that you have enough free space
on your ramdisk before you install too many of them.

Among the software you can install is a special *apt-get* wrap-
per that lets you install certain Debian packages; the F-Prot
virus scanner, so you can scan Windows systems; the Macro-
media Flash plug-in; the proprietary NVIDIA drivers, to
enable 3D acceleration of your video card; and a number of
games and other programs.

Create Boot Floppies

Not every computer has support for booting from CD-
ROMs. Luckily, Knoppix offers a script to automate the creation of floppies, which enables Knoppix to boot on these
systems. Older versions of Knoppix required that you either
use *dd* to write an image to a floppy, or use a Windows *.bat*
file. With the latest ISOLINUX boot method, boot floppy
creation methods have changed. One change is that you now
need two floppy disks.

To create the floppies, you need access to a second machine
that can boot Knoppix and has a floppy drive. Once Knoppix is booted, click K → KNOPPIX → Utilities → "Create
boot floppies for Knoppix." The script that appears will
prompt you to insert each floppy disk. Once the script has
finished, halt the machine and put the first floppy and the
CD-ROM into the machine you want to boot. The computer
will boot from the floppy drive, which will load a kernel
image, access your CD-ROM, and begin loading Knoppix.

Run Programs as Root

A common question among new Knoppix users is, "How do I run a program as root?" By default, Knoppix disables the root account completely. To run programs as root, use the *sudo* command. You might notice that many commands in this book are prefaced by the *sudo* command, which means that they require root permission. In a terminal window, type **sudo** in front of any command you wish to run with root privileges. For instance, use this command to run *fdisk* as root:

```
$ sudo fdisk
```

You can also click K → Knoppix → Root Shell to launch an xterm that already has root privileges.

Install Knoppix to the Hard Drive

Knoppix was originally intended to run from CD only, but even fairly early on, Knoppix users who saw how well the CD recognized and worked with their hardware wanted a way to install the system to a hard drive. Today, Knoppix provides a wizard that walks you through the process.

To start the Knoppix hard drive installer, type:

```
$ sudo knoppix-installer
```

The Knoppix installer has a few partition requirements that must be met:

- A Linux partition greater than 2 GB.
- A swap partition on systems with less than 512 MB RAM.

The wizard checks for these requirements and, if any are missing, launches a partitioning tool, so that you can create the necessary partitions.

With the partitions created, choose the Configure option. There are three different Knoppix install types you can choose from, each with its advantages and disadvantages:

Beginner

> This is the default method for installing Knoppix to a hard drive. With this option, Knoppix sets up a multiuser Debian system, but leaves all of the Knoppix hardware-detection scripts behind. You can still use most of the cheat codes at boot time and still have Knoppix run some of its hardware configuration scripts. This type of installation is a blend of the best features of the other two system types.

Knoppix

> This choice basically creates a copy of the live CD on your hard drive and allows you to boot from it. Just like the CD, this option installs only a single-user system with disabled passwords. Think of this option as running the Knoppix CD, only without the read-only restriction, so that you can install new software or updates, and more easily edit system files. Because passwords are disabled, this system type is potentially less secure than the other two.

Debian

> This choice offers a multiuser Debian install without any extra Knoppix hardware-detection scripts. The only cheat codes that will still work are those that are actually options passed to the kernel (such as those referenced in Table 5, earlier in the book). Think of this as the Beginner option without any of the hardware detection scripts. Experienced Knoppix users might recognize this as the same installation method provided by the old Knoppix installer scripts. Choose this option if you want to install a form of Knoppix that most closely resembles Debian.

The rest of the configuration process asks for information such as which partition to install onto and your username and password.

Once the configuration is finished, you are dropped back to the main menu. Click "Start installation" to actually proceed with the installation or "Save config" to save the configuration to the home directory, where it can be accessed later. The rest of the install process is automated, as Knoppix files are copied to the hard drive. Once the install finishes, reboot the machine and be sure to remove the Knoppix CD-ROM from the drive.

Image or Erase a Drive

Drive imaging is the process of taking a bit-for-bit copy of a drive or partition and transferring it to another drive, partition, or file. Imaging makes it easy to create an exact copy of a drive, which can be restored at a later date. Under Linux, *dd* is the tool commonly used for this process. Its basic arguments are an input file and an output file, and by default it uses *standard input* and *standard output* respectively if either option is missing. There are many different types of imaging you can perform with *dd*. Because *dd* is such a blunt tool, it doesn't take things for granted and will do exactly what you tell it. For instance, *dd* does not check whether the partition you image to is the same size as the partition you image from. If the sizes differ, *dd* will copy as much as it can before exiting. Also, *dd* does not split output into multiple files, nor does it compress files. For those functions, you will need to pipe the output of *dd* to other commands such as *split* and *gzip*. The following are some common imaging methods using *dd*.

Disk to disk:

```
$ sudo dd if=/dev/hda of=/dev/hdb
```

Partition to partition:

```
$ sudo dd if=/dev/hda1 of=/dev/hdb1
```

Partition to file:

```
$ sudo dd if=/dev/hda1 of=/mnt/hdb1/hda1_image.img
```

Master Boot Record to file:

```
$ sudo dd if=/dev/hda of=/mnt/hdb1/mbr.img bs=512 count=1
```

Partition to file over SSH:

```
$ sudo dd if=/dev/hda1 | ssh username@host \
"cat > /home/username/hda1_image.img"
```

To restore from an image, reverse the input and output files:

```
$ sudo dd if=/mnt/hdb1/hda1_image.img of=/dev/hda1
```

To restore over SSH, reverse the pipe:

```
$ ssh username@host "cat /home/username/hda1_image.img" \
| sudo dd of=/dev/hda1
```

Image a Damaged Drive

The *dd* utility works well enough for most imaging needs, but when a drive has bad blocks or other hardware errors, *dd* either exits with an error, or, if you use the noerror option, it outputs nothing for that block, potentially leaving you with a smaller output file than input file. This situation will cause problems if you try to mount the resulting file or reimage it to another drive.

For damaged drives, you need tools better suited to the task, such as *dd_rescue* and *dd_rhelp*. When *dd_rescue* finds an error on the drive, it retries multiple times to recover the block, and if it can't, it writes a zero to the output file for that location. The downside to *dd_rescue* is that it can be slow on drives with large clusters of bad blocks.

WARNING

The *dd_rescue* tool is not a drop-in replacement for *dd*, as the arguments and syntax have been changed. Don't use standard *dd* arguments with *dd_rescue* and expect them to work the same way.

The *dd_rhelp* utility works on the principle that bad blocks often are located in groups on a drive, and in the case of a recovery, you want to get all possible good data off the drive first, then try recovery of the bad blocks. *dd_rhelp* uses *dd_rescue*, but when it finds a bad block, it skips ahead until it finds a good block, then reads in reverse until it finds the end of the bad block. It keeps track of where it has been, and where groups of bad blocks are, so it can return to those spots later, after the majority of the good data has been recovered. This feature also means that *dd_rhelp* can be closed and resumed easily, and that it will pick up where it left off.

dd_rhelp and *dd_rescue* create a complete map of the drive being recovered in the recovery file, filling it with zeros in the place of blank data. When the program finds new data, it puts it in place of the zeros; you can thus treat the recovered file like an image at any point in the process. Just be aware that the longer you run *dd_rhelp*, the fewer blank holes (and therefore lost data) you will potentially have.

TIP

Because of how *dd_rhelp* works, it detects the size of the disk by trying to copy beyond the end-of-file (or EOF) on the disk. Usually it finds this location early on, but in the rare case that the end of the disk is full of bad sectors, it might take some time to find the EOF.

In this rare case, the recovery file won't be the exact size of the disk you are recovering until it finds the EOF, so give *dd_rhelp* extra time to run until it finds the EOF. It will show its detection of EOF at the bottom of its progress bar and in the report output.

There is a version of *dd_rescue* on Knoppix, but *dd_rhelp* requires a newer one. Download the Version 1.0.3 tar.gz file from *http://www.garloff.de/kurt/linux/ddrescue/*, extract the *dd_rescue* binary from the file, and move it to your *~/.dist/bin* directory:

```
$ mkdir -p ~/.dist/bin
$ tar xzf dd_rescue-1.03.tar.gz dd_rescue/dd_rescue
$ mv dd_rescue/dd_rescue ~/.dist/bin/
```

TIP

While any *dd_rescue* version newer than 1.0.3 will work with *dd_rhelp*, not all versions contain a precompiled binary. If your version doesn't, you'll have to compile the binary manually.

Grab the latest *dd_rhelp* file from *http://www.kalysto.ath.cx/utilities/dd_rhelp/index.en.html*, extract and compile it, and copy the compiled binary to *~/.dist/bin*:

```
$ tar xzf dd_rhelp-0.0.6.tar.gz
$ cd dd_rhelp-0.0.6/
$ ./configure && make
$ cp dd_rhelp ~/.dist/bin
```

You are now ready to run *dd_rhelp*. Mount the directory to store the image on with read/write permissions (in this example, */mnt/hdb1*), then run:

```
$ sudo dd_rhelp /dev/hda1 /mnt/hdb1/hda1_image.img
```

Replace *hda1* with the partition you are recovering. *dd_rhelp* will give you nice verbose output, so that you can follow its progress.

TIP

You can do a direct partition-to-partition image as well; just specify a partition instead of the path to a file as the second argument.

Once it is finished imaging, run *fsck* on the image to repair any damage to the filesystem:

```
$ sudo fsck -y /mnt/hdb1/hda1_image.img
```

Now you can mount the image loopback and examine the contents:

```
$ sudo mount -o loop /mnt/hdb1/hda1_image.img /mnt/temp
```

Replace **/mnt/temp** with the location to which you wish to mount the image. Alternatively, you can use *dd* to restore the image to a new drive.

Securely Erase Drives

Another use for *dd* is to erase data on drives and partitions. If you make */dev/zero* the input file (instead of an image), the output file will be completely overwritten with zeros:

```
$ sudo dd if=/dev/zero of=/dev/hda1
```

Because of the magnetic nature of hard drives, this type of drive erasing procedure isn't thorough enough to completely prevent data recovery from a determined individual. The more rigorous solution is to use the *shred* utility to overwrite the drive multiple times with various patterns of data. This command will overwrite the partition two times with patterns of data and a final time with zeros:

```
$ sudo shred -n 2 -z -v /dev/hda1
```

You can increase the value of -n to run more passes if you want to further ensure the data is irrecoverable. Table 12 lists other useful arguments to *shred*.

Table 12. Useful shred arguments for drives

Argument	Description
-n *n*	Overwrite *n* times instead of the default (25).
-v	Verbose output. Show progress.
-z	Add a final overwrite with zeros to hide shredding.
-	Shred standard output. Used to shred a removed temporary file.

Linux Security Response

When a computer has been broken into (or you suspect it has been broken into), a Knoppix CD doubles as a nice security response tool. Because Knoppix is so careful about mounting drives read-only by default, you can safely use it on compromised machines without worrying about whether it will overwrite valuable data.

Check for rootkits

Often, one of the first things an attacker does when he breaks into a Linux system is install a rootkit. A *rootkit* often modifies core utilities such as *ls*, *find*, *ps*, and other tools to hide its presence and provides a back door for the attacker to reenter the system. The *chkrootkit* tool is useful for searching for and identifying rootkits on the system, and it is made even more useful when run from a Knoppix CD, as you can be certain that the read-only CD has not been compromised, and that no hidden kernel modules or other processes are running.

To run *chkrootkit* from Knoppix, first mount the root directory you will scan, and then use the –r option to tell *chkrootkit* to use it as your root directory:

```
$ sudo chkrootkit -r /mnt/hda1
```

The output from *chkrootkit* will tell you what has been scanned and whether any rootkits have been discovered. Table 13 lists a number of other useful options for *chkrootkit*.

Table 13. Common chkrootkit arguments

Argument	Description
-l	Print available tests.
-x	Enter expert mode.
-q	Enter quiet mode.
-p	Specify the path for the external commands used by *chkrootkit* (useful if you suspect binaries on a system might be compromised).

Collect Forensics Data

When a system has been compromised, often the system administrator wants to analyze the system to determine how the attacker got in and possibly even the attacker's identity. While you can simply poke around a system looking for unusual files or system logs, doing so often destroys evidence—which is particularly problematic if you plan on prosecuting the attacker.

The Coroner's Toolkit (TCT), which contains a series of tools, aids in forensics analysis in a number of ways:

- It collects data according to the Order of Volatility, so data that might become volatile sooner (such as processes in RAM) is collected before less volatile data.

- It is automated. Automated processes reduce the chances for mistakes that can potentially destroy data.

- It collects a lot of data directly applicable for forensics analysis, including file access times and copies of important system files.

The best way to run TCT is from inside a running system, so that it can capture data about running processes. Unfortunately, if TCT isn't already installed on a system, installing it postcompromise increases the chance of destroying evidence. In this event, you will need to collect data from the system as a "corpse"—which is what TCT calls a halted system.

If possible, make an image of the compromised system and run the analysis from the image. This protects the actual system from mistakes and ensures that you can reimage it later for extra analysis. You will need both the drive (or an imaged drive) to examine and a second drive to store up to a few hundred megabytes of output.

Boot Knoppix with the noswap cheat code so that it will not automatically mount any swap drives it finds. Once Knoppix has booted, mount the corpse read-only and the drive that will store your data read/write. In this example, the corpse is */mnt/hda1* and the destination drive for output is */mnt/hdb1*. Create a directory (*/mnt/hdb1/data*, in this example) under the destination drive to store the output.

To gather forensics data, you will be using the *grave-robber* tool to automate the collection of data through other TCT tools. It is a good idea to run *grave-robber* from within a *script* session:

```
$ sudo script /mnt/hdb1/grave-robber-output
```

script saves all keystrokes and command output to a specified file, which means you have a log of each command you ran on the system and its output. You can now run *grave-robber* with the −v option so that verbose output will be saved in your *script* file.

```
root@0[knoppix]# grave-robber -c /mnt/hda1 -o LINUX2 \
-d /mnt/hdb1/data -v
```

Table 14 lists useful *grave-robber* arguments and their syntax. Once the command finishes, type **exit** to exit *script*.

Table 14. grave-robber arguments

Argument	Description
-b *body_file*	Write lstat and md5 information to this file instead of the default.
-c *corpse_dir*	Specify a dead, not live, system, such as a mounted disk.
-d *datadir*	Specify the data directory that stores all output files.
-o *os_type*	Specify what sort of corpse is being scanned. Choices include FREEBSD2, FREEBSD3, OPENBSD2, OPENBSD3, BSDI2, BSDI3, SUNOS4, SUNOS5, and LINUX2.
-v	Verbose output.

Once *grave-robber* has finished, a number of files and directories will appear within your data directory. Table 15 lists the major files and directories of interest.

Table 15. grave-robber output files

Filename	Description
body	Database of information for all files and directories on the system, including permissions, size, MAC times and other data.
body.S	Like body, but only contains SUID files for quick reference.
command_out	The output of various commands such as *df*, *dpkg/rpm*, and *lsof*.
conf_vault	A full copy of "interesting" files such as *./etc* configuration files.
pcat, icat, proc	Running process information. Useless when analyzing a corpse.
trust	*.forward*, *.rhosts*, and *crontab/at* output
user_vault	User shell histories, SSH keys, and so on.

Linux System Repair

Knoppix can be used as a rescue CD for Linux systems that no longer boot. Knoppix includes a number of tools that allow you to repair many of the common problems that prevent a system from booting. Many of the methods used with Knoppix to repair systems are applicable to a number of other repair CDs (such as Morphix, Knoppix-STD, and any other repair CD that contains the *chroot* tool).

Repair lilo and grub

A common use for a rescue CD is to restore a boot loader that has been either erased or loaded with incorrect options, leaving the system unbootable. The processes for restoring *lilo* and *grub* are pretty similar, as both use the *chroot* tool to run the installation program from within the host system.

TIP

There are other methods you can use to restore *lilo* or *grub*, but the *chroot* method is simpler, because it runs from within your installed Linux system. Any configuration files you have already created for your boot loader will automatically be referenced. It will act just as if you ran the commands from the running Linux system.

By default, Knoppix mounts all filesystems with the nodev option, which means that all device files (like you would find under */dev*) are deactivated. Because you will be installing the boot loader from within a *chroot* environment, these device files need to function, so the first step is to mount the root filesystem with the dev option:

```
$ sudo mount -o dev /dev/hda1 /mnt/hda1
```

Replace **hda1** with your root partition. If your system will no longer boot due to mistakes in your configuration file, now is the time to make any corrections (*/etc/lilo.conf* for *lilo* and */boot/grub/menu.lst* for *grub*). If for some reason your boot loader was corrupted or overwritten by some other boot loader (as can happen if you install Windows after you install Linux), your configuration file is probably fine, so you can move on to the next step.

Whether *lilo* is restored to the MBR or the beginning of a partition is determined by your */etc/lilo.conf* file. To restore *lilo* to the drive, type:

```
$ sudo chroot /mnt/hda1 lilo
```

Unlike with *lilo*, *grub-install* expects you to specify the drive to restore to from the command line (*/dev/hda* in this example). To restore *grub*, type:

```
$ sudo chroot /mnt/hda1 grub-install /dev/hda
```

Default lilo configuration

In case your entire */etc/lilo.conf* file was erased, here's a basic dual-boot configuration file to get started. Change all partitions to suit your system. In these examples, Windows is installed on */dev/hda1* and Linux is installed on */dev/hda2*:

```
# The hard drive to install lilo to
boot=/dev/hda
# The location of the lilo map file
map=/boot/map
```

```
# The location of the boot sector
install=/boot/boot.b
# Prompt with the lilo menu at boot
prompt
# Seconds to wait before booting default
timeout=10

# Linux configuration:
# Which kernel to boot
image=/boot/vmlinuz
# The label for this option
        label=linux
# The Linux root partition
        root=/dev/hda2

# Windows configuration:
# The location of the Windows partition
other=/dev/hda1
        label=windows
        table=/dev/hda
```

Default grub Configuration

In case */boot/grub/menu.lst* was erased, here is a default dual-boot *grub* configuration file. You can also enter these commands at a grub> prompt. Enter just the commands for a specific operating system to boot that operating system without a *grub* menu.

```
# boot the first entry by default
default 0
# Timeout after 10 seconds
timeout 10
# Fall back to second entry
fallback 1

# For booting Linux
# Name of menu option
title Linux
# Load /boot/vmlinuz kernel from /dev/hda2 (hd0,1)
# and make /dev/hda2 the root partition
kernel (hd0,1)/boot/vmlinuz root=/dev/hda2

# For booting Windows
title Windows
```

```
# Specify /dev/hda1 as the root partition
root (hd0,0)
# Set the active flag in the partition
makeactive
# Then boot the Windows boot loader
chainloader +1
```

The grub Command Line

You don't necessarily have to edit a *menu.lst* file from within
Knoppix to fix *grub*. If *grub* can't find a *menu.lst* file, you will
be dropped to a basic grub> prompt. This prompt is rather
powerful; you can access all of the *grub* options (listed next)
even without a menu.

boot

boot

Boot the OS or chain-loader that has already been loaded.

bootp

bootp

Initialize a network device via the BOOTP protocol.

cat

cat *file*

Display the contents of the specified file.

chainloader

chainloader [--force] *file*

Load *file* as a chainloader. Like any other file loaded by the filesystem code, it can use the blocklist notation to grab the first sector
of the current partition with +1. If you specify the option --force, it
will load *file* forcibly, whether it has a correct signature or not.

cmp

`cmp file1 file2`

Compare the specified files for differences in size or byte offset.

configfile

`configfile file`

Load specified file as a configuration file.

device

`device drive file`

Use the specified file as the actual drive for the specified BIOS
drive. Use to fix drives when *grub* guesses them incorrectly:

    grub> **device (hd0) /dev/sda**

displayapm

`displayapm`

Display APM BIOS information.

displaymem

`displaymem`

Display information about physical RAM.

find

`find filename`

Search for specified absolute filename (like */boot/grub/stage1*) in
all mountable partitions and print a list of which devices contain
the file.

halt

halt [--no-apm]

Halt the computer, using APM. If --no-apm is specified, no APM BIOS call is performed.

help

help [--all] [*pattern* ...]

Display help for commands. With no arguments, display a short description for most available commands. With --all option, display descriptions of rarely used commands as well. If patterns are specified, display verbose information about all commands matching the patterns.

hide

hide *partition*

Set the hidden bit in the partition type code to hide the specified partition. Useful for hiding multiple primary FAT partitions from Windows.

initrd

initrd *file*

Load a specified initial ramdisk for a Linux boot image.

kernel

kernel [--type=*type*] [--no-mem-option] *file* [*argument* ...]

Load the primary boot image from the specified file. Pass arguments after the specified file as kernel arguments. Use --type to specify the kernel type explicitly from netbsd, freebsd, openbsd, linux, biglinux, and multiboot options. The --no-mem-option argument is a Linux-only option that tells *grub* to not pass the mem= argument to the kernel.

makeactive

`makeactive`

Set the active partition on the root disk to *grub*'s root device.

map

`map to_drive from_drive`

Map *from_drive* to *to_drive*. Used when chainloading operating systems such as DOS that require they reside at the first drive. To swap the first two drives:

```
grub> map (hd0) (hd1)
grub> map (hd1) (hd0)
```

reboot

`reboot`

Reboot the computer.

root

`root device [hdbias]`

Set the current root device to the specified device, then try to mount it to get the partition size. The *hdbias* parameter is a number to tell a BSD kernel how many BIOS drive numbers are on controllers before the current one.

rootnoverify

`rootnoverify device [hdbias]`

Similar to the root command, only don't attempt to mount the specified device. Useful when an OS is outside an area of the disk that *grub* can read.

unhide

`unhide partition`

Unhide the specified hidden partition.

Repair Filesystem Errors

Knoppix includes all of the filesystem repair tools for the various Linux filesystems it supports including ext2, ext3, ReiserFS, XFS, and JFS. These tools might be used when a system was shut down improperly, or when major file-system damage occurred, such as in the case of a hardware error. In that condition, most filesystems require that they be repaired while unmounted.

In the case of a damaged root filesystem, you must use a res-cue CD such as Knoppix. The *fsck* utility acts as a frontend for filesystem-specific tools listed here. Certain filesystem types have slightly different methods for repair.

ext2/ext3

To check and repair errors:

```
$ sudo e2fsck /dev/hda1
```

e2fsck supports a number of arguments, the more useful of which are listed in Table 16.

Table 16. Some useful e2fsck arguments

Argument	Description
-b *superblock*	In the case of a corrupted primary superblock, use a backup superblock at the specified location.
-c	Run the *badblocks* program to find and mark any bad blocks on the filesystem.
-f	Force checking even if the filesystem seems clean.
-n	Report errors but do not repair them.
-p	Automatically repair the filesystem.

JFS

To check and repair JFS errors:

```
$ sudo jfs_fsck /dev/hda1
```

Table 17 lists some useful *jfs_fsck* options.

Table 17. Some useful jfs_fsck arguments

Argument	Description
-f	Replay the transaction log and force checking even if the filesystem appears clean. Repair all problems automatically.
-n	Report errors but do not repair them.
-p	Automatically repair the filesystem.

XFS

For XFS partitions, first check the filesystem for errors:

```
$ sudo xfs_check /dev/hda1
```

then repair, if any errors are found:

```
$ sudo xfs_repair /dev/hda1
```

Table 18 lists some common *xfs_repair* options.

Table 18. Some useful xfs_repair arguments

Argument	Description
-f	Specifies that the device is actually a file (as in the case of a drive image).
-n	No modify mode. Only scan the system and report what repairs would have been made.
-d	Repair dangerously. Allow *xfs_repair* to repair an XFS filesystem mounted read-only.

ReiserFS

For ReiserFS partitions, first check the filesystem for errors:

```
$ sudo reiserfsck --check /dev/hda1
```

If the check reports fixable errors:

```
$ sudo reiserfsck --fix-fixable /dev/hda1
```

If the check reports fatal corruptions, you might be facing some data loss. Image the partition elsewhere, if possible, and then rebuild the filesystem tree:

```
$ sudo reiserfsck --rebuild-tree /dev/hda1
```

In addition to these options, Table 19 lists other useful *reiserfsck* arguments.

Table 19. Some useful reiserfsck arguments

Argument	Description
--logfile *file*	Report any corruption to the specified file instead of *stderr*.
--nolog	Don't report any kind of corruption.
--quiet	Don't report the rate of progress.
--rebuild-sb	Rebuild the superblock for the filesystem.

The *fsck* tools have a common series of exit codes they return after completion. Table 20 lists these exit codes and their meanings:

Table 20. fsck exit codes

Exit code	Meaning
0	No errors.
1	Errors corrected.
2	Errors corrected; system should be rebooted.
4	Errors left uncorrected.
8	Operational error.
16	Usage or syntax error.
32	Canceled by user request.
128	Shared library error.

Restore a Partition Table

Many people assume that a corrupted partition table cannot be restored without having a backup. Luckily for those of us who don't back up our partition tables, there is *gpart*. *gpart* works by scanning the entire drive for filesystem signatures. It detects where filesystems begin and end, then reconstructs the partition table based on what it finds.

gpart works surprisingly well; however, it works best with primary partitions and can have trouble detecting extended partitions. Also, *gpart* isn't perfect. It sometimes doesn't detect the boundaries of a partition correctly, so you might have to go back and tweak what it finds.

To use *gpart*, first run the following command to scan the partition and see the results without making any changes:

```
$ sudo gpart /dev/hda
```

Replace **/dev/hda** with the name of your drive. If the output looks good, run this command to write the suggested changes to the drive:

```
$ sudo gpart -W /dev/hda /dev/hda
```

Though *gpart* gives you the option to make tweaks to what it has found from within the program, it is easier to write the changes and then go back with a tool like *fdisk* or *cfdisk* afterwards and make any needed corrections. The *gpart* utility also supports a number of other arguments, listed in Table 21.

Table 21. Useful gpart arguments

Argument	Description
-b *file*	If the –W option (see entry later in this table) is specified, and the guessed partition table is to be written, back up the current partition table to the specified file.
-C *c,h,s*	Set the disk geometry (cylinders, heads, sectors) for the scan. Useful if the disk to be scanned was partitioned using a different geometry.
-E	Don't try to identify extended partition tables.
-f	Full scan. When a possible partition is found, *gpart* normally skips all sectors that this entry seems to occupy and continues the scan from the end of the last possible partition.

Table 21. Useful gpart arguments (continued)

Argument	Description
-g	Don't try to get the disk geometry from the OS. Useful when scanning a disk image.
-i	Scan interactively. Ask the user for confirmation each time a partition is identified.
-q	Quiet mode. No output is given.
-W *device*	Write partition table to specified device.

TIP

You don't have to have a damaged partition table to use *gpart*. You could use *gpart* without the -W option just to test how *gpart* would be able to recover your partition table.

---

chroot into Systems

The *chroot* utility allows you to run commands from a mounted filesystem as though it were the root filesystem. Used from a Knoppix CD, *chroot* allows you to perform many changes on a broken system or unbootable system to get it back up and running.

Before you use *chroot*, be sure to mount the filesystem correctly. By default, Knoppix mounts filesystems read-only and with the nodev option, so that device files are disabled. For many *chroot* uses, you need a read/write filesystem with a functioning /dev filesystem, so mount the drive from the command line with these special options:

```
$ sudo mount -o rw,dev /dev/hda1 /mnt/hda1
```

chroot accepts as arguments a directory to set to root and, optionally, a command to run. With only a directory as an argument, *chroot* drops you to a shell within the new root:

```
knoppix@ttyp1[knoppix]$ sudo chroot /mnt/hda1
root@Knoppix:/#
```

You can type commands within this shell—they will run just as if you had booted into /mnt/hda1 directly. Type **exit** to leave *chroot*.

If you specify a command as an argument to *chroot*, it will change to the new root directory, run the command, and then exit automatically. This trick can be useful for quick commands, such as restoring *lilo* and *grub*, described earlier.

You can also use a *chroot* environment to perform package management on a mounted partition. *chroot* into the directory, then run *rpm* or *dpkg* as normal.

If you want to run graphical programs from *chroot*, you need to perform an additional step. Since graphical programs need access to your current X session, you must mount your current /tmp directory onto the /tmp directory inside your *chroot* environment:

```
knoppix@ttyp1[knoppix]$ sudo mount --bind /tmp \
/mnt/hda1/tmp
```

Now run *chroot* and type the name of the graphical program you wish to run. Your current DISPLAY environment variable will carry over.

General Hardware Probing

Listed here are some standard Linux commands that you can use to probe your hardware. Linux is pretty open about telling you what it knows about the hardware on your system, provided you know how to ask and where to look.

At boot time, quite a bit of data about the hardware on a system scrolls by, only to be replaced by the desktop. This information can be accessed with the *dmesg* command; it contains valuable information including PCI and IDE devices detected by the kernel at boot.

```
knoppix@ttyp0[knoppix]$ dmesg
...
AMD7411: 00:07.1 (rev 01) UDMA100 controller
```

```
    ide0: BM-DMA at 0xf000-0xf007, BIOS settings: hda:DMA,
hdb:DMA
    ide1: BM-DMA at 0xf008-0xf00f, BIOS settings: hdc:pio,
hdd:pio
hda: WDC WD1000BB-00CAA1, ATA DISK drive
hdb: WDC WD300BB-00AUA1, ATA DISK drive
hdc: SAMSUNG DVD-ROM SD-612, ATAPI CD/DVD-ROM drive
...
usb.c: registered new driver hiddev
usb.c: registered new driver hid
input: USB HID v1.00 Mouse [Microsoft Microsoft
IntelliMouse® Explorer] on usb1:2.0
...
Linux Tulip driver version 0.9.15-pre12 (Aug 9, 2002)
eth0: Lite-On PNIC-II rev 37 at 0x1000, 00:A0:CC:32:BF:88,
IRQ 5.
...
```

TIP

Because it produces a lot of output, you might want to
pipe *dmesg* through a pager such as *less* for easier reading:

```
$ dmesg | less
```

Linux also provides the *lspci* command to list the information Linux has about your PCI devices. With no additional
arguments, *lspci* will list basic information about the hardware on a system:

```
knoppix@ttyp0[knoppix]$ sudo lspci
0000:00:00.0 Host bridge: Advanced Micro Devices [AMD]
AMD-760 MP [IGD4-2P]
System Controller (rev 11)
0000:00:01.0 PCI bridge: Advanced Micro Devices [AMD] AMD-
760 MP [IGD4-2P]
AGP Bridge
0000:00:07.0 ISA bridge: Advanced Micro Devices [AMD] AMD-
766 [ViperPlus]
ISA (rev 02)
0000:00:07.1 IDE interface: Advanced Micro Devices [AMD]
AMD-766 [ViperPlus]
IDE (rev 01)
0000:00:07.3 Bridge: Advanced Micro Devices [AMD] AMD-766
[ViperPlus] ACPI
```

```
(rev 01)
0000:00:07.4 USB Controller: Advanced Micro Devices [AMD]
AMD-766 [ViperPlus]
USB (rev 07)
0000:00:0c.0 Ethernet controller: Lite-On Communications
Inc LNE100TX [Linksys
EtherFast 10/100] (rev 25)
0000:00:0d.0 Multimedia audio controller: Aureal
Semiconductor Vortex 2
0000:01:05.0 VGA compatible controller: nVidia Corporation
NV11 [GeForce2 MX/MX
400] (rev a1)
```

TIP

Add the -vv argument to *lspci* to see extremely verbose
output about all of your PCI devices.

Use *ifconfig* to list information about the current network
configuration:

```
knoppix@ttyp0[knoppix]$ /sbin/ifconfig
          eth0 Link encap:Ethernet HWaddr 00:A0:CC:32:BF:88
          inet addr:192.168.0.2  Bcast:192.168.0.255
Mask:255.255.255.0
          UP BROADCAST RUNNING MULTICAST  MTU:1500
Metric:1
          RX packets:3927 errors:0 dropped:0 overruns:0
frame:0
          TX packets:3240 errors:1 dropped:0 overruns:0
carrier:2
          collisions:0 txqueuelen:1000
          RX bytes:5278944 (5.0 MiB)  TX bytes:1692461
(1.6 MiB)
          Interrupt:5 Base address:0x1000

lo        Link encap:Local Loopback
          inet addr:127.0.0.1  Mask:255.0.0.0
          UP LOOPBACK RUNNING  MTU:16436  Metric:1
          RX packets:16 errors:0 dropped:0 overruns:0
frame:0
          TX packets:16 errors:0 dropped:0 overruns:0
carrier:0
          collisions:0 txqueuelen:0
          RX bytes:896 (896.0 b)  TX bytes:896 (896.0 b)
```

Windows System Repair

While it may seem intuitive that Knoppix can be used to repair Linux systems, many people are surprised to learn that Knoppix is also an effective Windows repair tool. Knoppix can read and write to FAT and FAT32 partitions natively, and to NTFS partitions by using the Captive NTFS program.

On the CD are a number of programs you can use for Windows system repair, and even more are available with a quick download. Here are some common repair scenarios and how to use Knoppix to remedy them.

Back Up Important Files

A common response to a broken Windows system is to format the drive and reinstall Windows. If you decide to go this (rather drastic) route, you might want to back up your important files beforehand. Windows organizes files into a few major locations, and this method makes it easier to target the files that are important for you to save.

Knoppix will automatically put a hard drive icon on the desktop to represent each partition it detects when it boots. You can click on the hard drive icon to mount it and explore the contents of the drive for data you want to back up. Once you find the data you want to back up, you can drag and drop files to a USB drive or to a directory shared over the network, or even burn them to a CD. Here are the major directories in the root of a Windows filesystem:

Documents and Settings
> The *Documents and Settings* directory contains all of the personal user directories for every user on the system. Inside each user directory you will find your *Desktop* directory, the *My Documents* and *My Pictures* directories, and directories that contain personal settings and configuration data for that user.

Program Files

> The *Program Files* directory holds executable files and libraries for most of the programs installed on your system. These programs are organized into directories that are typically named by the company who produced the software. Generally, it is easier to reinstall a program than to back up this directory and copy it to a fresh install—plus, in many cases, the program won't work after copying it to a new system. There are, however, some files that might be worth backing up in this directory, such as saved game data.

Windows (or WINNT)

> This directory holds all of the system files, executables, and libraries that your system needs. Generally, these files will be restored when you reinstall Windows, so there isn't much worth backing up here.

Write to FAT and FAT32

Knoppix has native support for reading from and writing to FAT and FAT32 partitions. To mount a drive from the desktop, click the corresponding hard drive icon. To unmount it, right-click on the hard drive icon and choose Unmount. By default, Knoppix mounts a drive as read-only. To mount it as read/write, right-click an already mounted drive and choose Actions → "Change read/write mode."

Mounting a drive from the console is almost as simple as doing so from the desktop. To mount a drive with the default option of read-only, type this command:

```
$ mount /mnt/hda1
```

Replace *hda1* with the name of your partition. To mount a drive as read/write, type:

```
$ mount -o rw /mnt/hda1
```

To unmount a drive, type:

```
$ umount /mnt/hda1
```

Write to NTFS

While the Linux kernel can currently mount and read NTFS partitions, it cannot reliably write to them the way that it can to FAT and FAT32 filesystems. You can, however, write to NTFS under Linux using the Captive NTFS utility. This utility uses the NTFS *.dll* files that Windows itself uses.

Knoppix includes a wizard to ease the configuration of Captive NTFS. Click K → KNOPPIX → Utilities → Captive NTFS to launch the program. Click through the steps in the wizard to scan your complete system for usable drivers. If it can't find the drivers it needs, you have the option to point it to drivers it can use, or to have the wizard download the files from Windows XP Service Pack 1.

WARNING

Windows XP Service Pack 2 files have been known to break Captive NTFS, so if you have upgraded to Service Pack 2, you need to have the wizard download the files from Service Pack 1.

Once the wizard has found files that it can use, you must mount the filesystem from the command line, so that you can pass special options to the mount command, like this:

```
$ sudo mount -t captive-ntfs -o uid=knoppix,gid=knoppix \
/dev/hda1 /mnt/hda1
```

Writing to NTFS with this method can be rather slow, so keep that in mind if you intend to write large files. Once you are finished writing to the partition, be sure to unmount it:

```
$ sudo umount /mnt/hda1
```

WARNING

You must unmount the partition before you reboot Knoppix to make sure any changes you have made are synced. Failure to do so risks losing any changes you have made to the drive.

If you would like to save all of the Captive NTFS files and *.dlls* you have found so that you only have to search for them once, this command will create a special *configs.tbz* file that you can use with a *knoppix.sh* file from the *saveconfig* script:

```
$ BZIP2=-9 sudo tar -cpPjf configs.tbz \
/home/knoppix/.dist/ \
/home/knoppix/.knx-live-inst/ \
/home/knoppix/Software/ \
/home/knoppix/Desktop/Extra\ Software/ \
/var/lib/captive/*.sys \
/var/lib/captive/ntoskrnl.exe
```

Scan for Viruses

When a system is infected with a virus, it can sometimes be difficult to tell what damage was done or whether you are fully rid of the infection. You can boot Knoppix on an infected Windows machine and scan it for viruses. Doing this ensures that the Windows machine won't try to infect other machines while powered on, and prevents the virus from taking steps to avoid detection. The F-Prot virus scanning tool does not come preinstalled on the Knoppix CD, but you can easily get it using the Knoppix live software install tool. Click K → KNOPPIX → Utilities → "Install software" and select F-Prot from the list. Click K → KNOPPIX → Extra Software → F-Prot to start the F-Prot GUI.

The first step is to click Do Online-Update to make sure you have the latest virus definitions. Then click "Select partition(s)" to choose which partitions to scan, and Scan to start the scanning process.

The scanning process will take some time; once it is finished, a text file will appear with the output. At the bottom of the file will be a set of statistics telling you the number of infected files.

Once you have identified infected files, you may choose to mount the filesystem read/write and manually delete the files; rename them; or back them up to a safe location. Remember that if you have an NTFS partition, you will have to use Captive NTFS to mount the partition as read/write.

Edit the Windows Registry

One of the surprising things you can do with Knoppix is edit the Windows Registry. The *chntpw* utility makes this possible, and although Knoppix doesn't include this tool out of the box, it can be downloaded and installed once Knoppix is booted.

The simplest way to get *chntpw* under Knoppix is to extract the binary from the corresponding Debian package. Download the latest *.deb* for *chntpw* from *http://packages.debian.org/unstable/ admin/chntpw*, extract the binary, and move it to *~/.dist/bin/* (which is in your path). (Create the *~/.dist/bin* directory if it doesn't exist.) Here are the commands to do this:

```
$ alien --to-tgz chntpw_0.99.2-1_i386.deb
$ tar xvzf chntpw_0.99.2.tgz ./usr/sbin/chntpw
$ mv ./usr/sbin/chntpw ~/.dist/bin/
```

Reset Windows passwords

The primary use for *chntpw* is to reset Windows passwords. Mount your Windows partition read/write and then find the SAM Registry hive, which should be located under *Windows/ System32/Config* or *WinNT/System32/Config*. If you run *chntpw*

with only the path to the SAM hive as an argument, it defaults
to resetting the administrator password:

```
$ chntpw windows/system32/config/SAM
```

To reset a different user, use the –u option:

```
$ chntpw -u username windows/system32/config/SAM
```

TIP

Be sure to unmount the Windows directory to ensure that
any changes are synced.

Change other Registry settings

chntpw is not limited to just changing password settings: you
can use it to browse, modify, and add keys throughout the
Windows Registry. This tool can be particularly useful if you
need to remove Registry keys in order to fully remove a virus or
worm from a Windows machine.

First, you need to decide which Registry hive file contains the
key you want to change. The Registry is split up into a number of files, as Table 22 illustrates. Most of the files can be
found under *Windows\System32\Config* or *WinNT\System32\
Config*, except for *NTuser.dat*, found under *Documents and
Settings\<username>*.

Table 22. Registry keys and their corresponding hive file

Registry key name	Filename
HKEY_CURRENT_CONFIG	*SYSTEM*
HKEY_CURRENT_USER	*NTuser.dat*
HKEY_LOCAL_MACHINE\SAM	*SAM*
HKEY_LOCAL_MACHINE\SECURITY	*SECURITY*
HKEY_LOCAL_MACHINE\SOFTWARE	*SOFTWARE*
HKEY_USERS\DEFAULT	*DEFAULT*

Once you have identified the file to edit, run *chntpw* with the -e argument to browse that hive interactively:

```
$ chntpw -e SOFTWARE
```

WARNING

Editing the Registry can be a dangerous and potentially destructive proposition. Back up any Registry hives before you edit them.

The interface is somewhat like a DOS or Linux shell and allows you to browse through keys as though they were directories and files. Table 23 lists *chntpw* shell commands and their functions.

Table 23. chntpw shell commands

Command	Function
hive [*n*]	List loaded hives or switch to hive number *n*
cd *key*	Change to *key*
ls | dir [*key*]	Show subkeys and values
cat | type *value*	Show key value
st [*hexaddr*]	Show struct information
nk *keyname*	Add key
dk *keyname*	Delete key
ed *value*	Edit value
nv *type value*	Add value
dv *value*	Delete value
Delallv	Delete all values in current key
Debug	Enter buffer hex editor
Q	Quit
?	Show help

Once you are finished editing the Registry, unmount the file-system to ensure that the changes are synced.

Remaster Knoppix

Knoppix includes a lot of different kinds of software on the CD; the base CD is a good general-purpose distribution. Knoppix's design also makes it a great base distribution to create (also known as *remastering*) your own live CD. You might want to do this so that you can include software that isn't already on the Knoppix CD, or because you want to create your own very custom live CD distribution and don't want to start from scratch.

The remastering process looks complex, but is pretty simple once you get the hang of it. The basic process is to copy the current Knoppix system to disk, *chroot* into it, change the system to how you would like it, and then create a new CD image based on the new system.

Remastering Knoppix requires a lot of hard drive space to store the contents of the CD. The partition doesn't have to be completely empty, but you do need around 4.5 GB of free space (less if you don't need to create a swap file). The partition must be formatted with a Linux filesystem, so that file permissions are preserved during the remastering process.

Because basically every command involved in this process requires root permissions, you might find that it's easier to launch a root shell (K → KNOPPIX → Root Shell) instead of prefacing every command with **sudo**.

Mount the partition that will hold your remaster read/write and with the dev option and change to that directory. The majority of commands for the remastering process take place within this directory. Here are the commands for this:

```
root@ttyp1[knoppix]# mount -o rw,dev /dev/hda1 /mnt/hda1
root@ttyp1[knoppix]# cd /mnt/hda1
```

If you have less than a gigabyte of RAM, you need to create a temporary swap file so that you have enough memory for the remastering process.

TIP

Remember that Knoppix will use any swap partitions it detects at boot time, so if you have a large enough swap partition, you can skip creating a swap file.

You can vary the size of the swap file depending on how much RAM you have, but to create a 750MB swap file, first create a blank 750MB file:

```
root@ttyp1[hda1]# dd if=/dev/zero of=swapfile bs=1M \
count=750
```

Format the file with the swap filesystem and then add it to your swap storage:

```
root@ttyp1[hda1]# mkswap swapfile
root@ttyp1[hda1]# swapon swapfile
```

Prepare the Source Filesystem

The Knoppix remastering process takes advantage of *chroot* so that you can make any changes to the filesystem that you would want, such as adding or removing packages or changing configuration files. To make changes, create a directory called *source* and copy all 2.2 GB of the uncompressed Knoppix filesystem to it using these commands:

```
root@ttyp1[hda1]# mkdir source
root@ttyp1[hda1]# mkdir source/KNOPPIX
root@ttyp1[hda1]# cp -Rp /KNOPPIX/* source/KNOPPIX
```

The *source/KNOPPIX* directory should look like the root of a standard Debian filesystem. The next step is to *chroot* into this directory, but first you will want to copy over some network configuration files that Knoppix created at boot time, so the *chroot* environment can resolve domain names:

```
root@ttyp1[hda1]# cp /etc/dhcpc/resolv.conf \
source/KNOPPIX/etc/dhcpc/resolv.conf
```

TIP

You can also copy other necessary configuration files created at boot time, such as */etc/samba/smb.conf* for Samba.

---

chroot into the *source/KNOPPIX* directory and mount the *proc* filesystem to give you access to the network and other kernel interfaces:

```
root@ttyp1[hda1]# chroot source/KNOPPIX
root@ttyp1[/]# mount -t proc /proc proc
```

When you are finished making all of your changes to the source filesystem, unmount the *proc* filesystem:

```
root@ttyp1[/]# umount /proc
```

and press Ctrl-D to exit *chroot*.

Package Management

The primary thing that most remastered CDs change from standard Knoppix is the set of packages. The Knoppix CD is cramped for space, so you will need to remove packages from the system to make room for newer packages. To find out which packages are taking the most space, run this command:

```
root@ttyp0[/]# dpkg-query -W \
--showformat='${Installed-Size} ${Package}\n' | sort -n
```

To remove a package, use *apt-get*:

```
root@ttyp0[/]# apt-get --purge remove packagename
```

The --purge option will also remove any associated configuration files—because we are concerned about space, every
kilobyte counts. Removing a package often also removes
packages that depend on that package. To see a list of depen-
dencies for a package, type:

```
root@ttyp0[/]# apt-cache rdepends packagename | uniq
```

Remove orphans

If you have been remastering for some time, you will likely
want to remove any orphaned packages from your remaster.
Orphans are packages (usually libraries) on which no other
packages depend. To list all orphaned libraries sorted by size,
run this command:

```
root@ttyp0[/]# deborphan -z | sort -n
```

To automatically remove all orphans from your system, use
this command:

```
root@ttyp0[/]# deborphan | xargs apt-get -y --purge remove
```

Add packages

Once you have cleared up some space on your filesystem for
new packages, run this command to get the latest list of
packages for your system:

```
root@ttyp0[/]# apt-get update
```

Then upgrade your installed programs:

```
root@ttyp0[/]# apt-get upgrade
```

To add new packages to the system, search for the name of the package you want to install:

```
root@ttyp1[/]# apt-cache search keyword
```

Use the following command to install the package:

```
root@ttyp1[/]# apt-get install packagename
```

Once you have finished making all changes to the filesystem, remove the downloaded package files with this command:

```
root@ttyp1[/]# apt-get clean
```

If you are making a lot of changes and have only a limited amount of free space under the 700MB CD image limit, you might need to run **apt-get clean** as an intermediate step to free up space to install the next program.

Interesting Configuration Files

There are a number of configuration files that are of interest if you are remastering Knoppix. These files tweak settings within Knoppix, often in ways that you might not be used to with a normal Linux distribution. You generally won't have to be within the *chroot* environment to edit any of these files—just make sure that you edit the version of the file that is within the *source/KNOPPIX* directory. Described here are some of the special configuration files and what they do.

/etc/init.d/knoppix-autoconfig

This script manages a lot of what happens between Knoppix booting and the desktop environment scripts loading. All of the Knoppix cheat codes that aren't kernel parameters (such as myconfig and lang) are interpreted here.

/etc/init.d/xsession

Like */etc/X11/Xsession.d/45xsession*, this file controls much of what happens when Knoppix launches and shuts down X, including detecting and loading special graphical modules. This file also controls the sound that plays when you shut down the computer.

/etc/X11/Xsession.d/45xsession

This file controls much of what happens when X loads. It specifies which desktop environment to load and what happens when a particular desktop environment is loaded, so if you want to add extra desktop environments to Knoppix or tweak what Knoppix does when it boots a desktop environment, look to this file.

For instance, to disable the sound that Knoppix makes when it loads the desktop, find the following lines, and make sure that the playsound option is commented out:

```
playsound( ){
# Play sound if soundcore module present (checking
/dev/syndstat is unreliable)
...
}
```

Comment out all of the lines in between the two braces.

Most of this script has documentation that tells you what different sections of the script do, but there are also a few other sections of this file that might be of particular interest. Find the comment in the code that says:

```
# Copy profiles if not already present
```

Below this comment are a series of *rsync* commands that perform the initial synchronization between the */etc/skel* directory and */home/knoppix*. If you need to add other configuration files that this section doesn't cover, this is a good place to add them.

Near the middle of the script are a number of shell functions that have the name start*windowmanager*, such as startkde, startwindowmaker, startfluxbox, and others. Inside each of these functions are the different commands that Knoppix executes when that particular desktop is selected. This is a good section to go to if you just want to change something Knoppix does for a particular window manager.

/etc/sysconfig/desktop

This file might or might not exist by default on your remaster. If it does, Knoppix will load the desktop specified in the file, instead of the default desktop from *etc/X11/Xsession.d/ 45xsession*. For instance, to change the default desktop to *fluxbox*, make sure this file contains the line:

```
DESKTOP="fluxbox"
```

TIP

This file is overridden if the user enters the desktop cheat code at boot time.

/etc/skel

A common remastering mistake is to edit the default user configuration files from within the */home* directory. Knoppix actually stores all the files for the default Knoppix user under */etc/ skel* and copies these files to */home/knoppix* when the desktop is launched. If you look inside the */etc/X11/Xsession.d/45xsession* file, you will find the *rsync* commands that perform the synchronization.

If you want to change the default user desktop, make changes to your settings in the home directory, where it's simpler, and then copy the changes to the */etc/skel* directory.

To synchronize all of the user settings with the *letc/skel* directory, make sure you are out of the *chroot* environment, and run this command:

```
knoppix@ttyp0[knoppix]$ sudo rsync -a /home/knoppix/ \
/mnt/hda1/source/KNOPPIX/etc/skel/
```

Replace */mnt/hda1* with the path to your *source/KNOPPIX* directory.

Make the Master CD Filesystem

After the *source* directory is prepared, create a *master* directory next to it. This directory will hold the files that will be converted into an ISO-9660 CD-ROM filesystem. Copy all of the files from the CD itself to the *master* directory, excluding the *KNOPPIX/KNOPPIX* compressed filesystem, using these commands:

```
root@ttyp1[hda1]# mkdir master
root@ttyp1[hda1]# rsync -a --exclude "/KNOPPIX/KNOPPIX" \
/cdrom/ master/
```

Now create your custom *KNOPPIX/KNOPPIX* file. This file is actually a highly compressed filesystem that is created from the *source/KNOPPIX* directory. Use this command to make the file:

```
root@ttyp1[hda1]# mkisofs -R -U -V "Knoppix Pocket" \
-P "Knoppix Pocket" -hide-rr-moved -cache-inodes -no-bak \
-pad source/KNOPPIX | nice -5 \
/usr/bin/create_compressed_fs - 65536 \
> master/KNOPPIX/KNOPPIX
```

This command will take some time to finish; it averages about 30 minutes on a 1.2Ghz system. Table 24 lists some of the common *mkisofs* options.

Table 24. mkisofs options

Argument	Description
-b *boot_image*	Specifies the path and filename of the boot image to be used when making a bootable CD.
-c *boot_catalog*	Specifies the path and filename of the boot catalog to be used when making an "El Torito" bootable CD.
-l	Allow full 31-character filenames.
-o *filename*	The name of the file to which the ISO-9660 filesystem image should be written.
-r	Like the -R option, but with file ownership and modes set to more useful values. The *uid* and *gid* are set to zero, because they are generally useful only on the author's system, and not useful to the client.
-v	Verbose execution.
-J	Generate Joliet directory records in addition to regular ISO-9660 filenames. This option is useful primarily when the disks are to be used on Windows NT or Windows 95 machines.
-R	Generate SUSP and RR records using the Rock Ridge protocol to further describe the files on the ISO-9660 filesystem.
-U	Allows "untranslated" filenames, completely violating the ISO-9660 standards. It allows more than one "." character in the filename, as well as mixed-case filenames.
-V *volumeid*	Specifies the volume ID to be written into the master block. Up to 32 characters can be used.
-P	Get POSIX.1-2001 semantics with mkisofs-2.02.
-boot-info-table	Specifies that a 56-byte table with information on the CD-ROM layout will be patched in at offset eight in the boot file.
-hide-rr-moved	Rename the *RR_MOVED* directory to *.rr_moved* to help hide it from users who might not know what the *RR_MOVED* directory is for.
-cache-inodes	Cache inode and device numbers to find hard links to files. If *mkisofs* finds a hard link (a file with multiple names), then the file will appear only once on the CD, to save space.
-no-bak	Do not include backup files (files that contain ~, #, or end in *.bak*) on the CD.

Table 24. mkisofs options (continued)

Argument	Description
-no-emul-boot	Specifies that the boot image used to create "El Torito" bootable CDs is a "no emulation" image. The system will load and execute this image without performing any disk emulation.
-pad	Pad the end of the whole image by 150 sectors. Needed to avoid problems with I/O errors on the last file on the filesystem under some operating systems.

TIP

If your *KNOPPIX* file isn't compressing small enough, you can add the --best option after the */usr/bin/create_compressed_fs* command to increase the compression even more (and also increase the time it takes to complete).

Files on the Knoppix CD

With the compressed filesystem created, you can edit other files within the *master* directory. Listed here are the files contained on the CD image, and their functions.

KNOPPIX/KNOPPIX

This is the heavily compressed Knoppix root filesystem. More than 2 GB of files are stored here.

KNOPPIX/KNOPPIX_FAQ*.txt

Contains answers to frequently asked questions about Knoppix in multiple languages.

KNOPPIX/background.png

This file is the background image Knoppix uses on the desktop. Its placement in this directory makes it easy to customize the background image for a CD without having to fully remaster. Change this file and then burn a copy of the CD.

KNOPPIX/index*.html
>An introductory Knoppix HTML page in multiple languages.

KNOPPIX/images/*
>A directory containing images for the introductory Knoppix HTML page.

KNOPPIX/knoppix-cheatcodes.txt
>This file contains the latest list of cheat codes for the Knoppix CD, along with some instructions on their use.

KNOPPIX/knoppix-version
>The official version for this Knoppix CD.

KNOPPIX/md5sums
>A list of MD5sums for files on the CD. Used with the testcd cheat code to verify that the CD is error-free.

autorun.pif
>This executable, together with its configuration file, *autorun.inf*, manages what happens when the Knoppix CD is inserted in a Windows machine with autorun enabled.

autorun.inf
>This is the configuration file for autorun; specifies what to execute when the Knoppix CD is inserted and which CD-ROM icon to use.

autorun.bat
>This batch file is executed by autorun when Knoppix is inserted into a Windows CD-ROM drive. It opens up the *index.html* file with the default HTML viewer. Edit this file if you want to change autorun behavior.

cdrom.ico
>The CD-ROM icon that appears on Windows.

index.html

The HTML file that appears when the Knoppix CD is inserted in Windows.

boot/isolinux/boot*

Configuration files for the messages that appear at the boot: prompt.

boot/isolinux/f2*

Determines the messages that appear at the boot: prompt when you hit F2.

boot/isolinux/f3*

Determines the messages that appear at the boot: prompt when you hit F3.

boot/isolinux/german.kbd

German keyboard settings.

boot/isolinux/isolinux.bin

The ISOLINUX boot loader for the CD.

boot/isolinux/isolinux.cfg

Configuration settings for ISOLINUX. This file contains each of the possible kernel options for the boot: prompt and what they do. It also controls which files are referenced for the boot messages. The first couple of lines of the file will give you a clue as to the sorts of things that you can change with this file:

```
DEFAULT linux24
APPEND ramdisk_size=100000 init=/etc/init lang=us \
apm=power-off vga=791 initrd=minirt24.gz nomce quiet \
BOOT_IMAGE=knoppix
TIMEOUT 300

PROMPT 1
DISPLAY boot.msg
F1 boot.msg
F2 f2
F3 f3
LABEL knoppix
KERNEL linux24
APPEND ramdisk_size=100000 init=/etc/init lang=us \
```

```
apm=power-off vga=791 initrd=minirt24.gz nomce quiet \
BOOT_IMAGE=knoppix
LABEL linux26
KERNEL linux26
APPEND ramdisk_size=100000 init=/etc/init lang=us \
apm=power-off vga=791 initrd=minirt26.gz nomce \
BOOT_IMAGE=knoppix
...
```

boot/isolinux/linux24

>The 2.4 Linux kernel image.

boot/isolinux/linux26

>The 2.6 Linux kernel image.

boot/isolinux/logo.16

>The ISOLINUX-compatible logo that appears on the boot screen. To edit this image, copy it to a temporary location and convert it to PPM format, so that you can edit it with a program, such as the GIMP.

>```
># lss16toppm < logo.16 > logo.ppm
>```

>Once you are finished editing the image, convert it back to its original format and copy it back to *boot/isolinux/*.

>```
># ppmtolss16 < logo.ppm > logo.16
>```

boot/isolinux/memtest

>The Memtest86+ kernel.

boot/isolinux/minirt24.gz and minirt25.gz

>These two files are a compressed miniature root partition that the kernel mounts initially. You can copy these files to your local directory, then decompress and mount them loopback using these commands:

>```
>root@ttyp1[hda1]# cp master/boot/isolinux/minirt*.gz .
>root@ttyp1[hda1]# gunzip minirt24.gz
>root@ttyp1[hda1]# mkdir temp
>root@ttyp1[hda1]# mount -t ext2 -o loop minirt24 /temp
>```

>Once it is mounted, you will see a small version of the root filesystem within the temporary directory. You can then edit files inside it; specifically, the *linuxrc* file, which is the init script for Knoppix. That script contains many

of the commands Knoppix runs at boot time. After you have made your changes, unmount the temporary directory, compress the file, then copy it back to the *master/* filesystem using these commands:.

```
root@ttyp1[hda1]# umount temp
root@ttyp1[hda1]# gzip minirt24
root@ttyp1[hda1]# cp minirt24.gz master/boot/isolinux/
```

Regenerate checksums

After you have made all of your changes, the final step before creating the CD image is to regenerate the list of Knoppix checksums:

```
root@ttyp1[hda1]# cd master
root@ttyp1[master]# rm -f KNOPPIX/md5sums
root@ttyp1[master]# find -type f -not -name md5sums \
-not -name boot.cat -exec md5sum {} \; >> KNOPPIX/md5sums
root@ttyp1[master]# cd ..
```

Create the CD image

Now the CD image is ready to be generated. This step requires one final (but relatively quick) *mkisofs* command:

```
root@ttyp1[hda1]# mkisofs -pad -l -r -J -v -V "KNOPPIX" \
no-emul-boot -boot-load-size 4 -boot-info-table \
-b boot/isolinux/isolinux.bin -c boot/isolinux/boot.cat \
-hide-rr-moved -o knoppix.iso master/
```

This command creates a new *knoppix.iso* file in the root of your partition. You can either burn this directly to a CD-ROM or use the bootfrom cheat code to try it out first.

Experimental Features

As this book is being written, Knoppix 3.8 has been released with a few rather interesting features and changes. Because these features are so new and aren't even available in an official download version of Knoppix, I consider them experimental and subject to future change. That said, here I will document some of the new features in Knoppix 3.8.

UnionFS

From its creation, Knoppix was designed to be used as a day-to-day portable Linux distribution. Over time, a number of scripts have been created to help you to maintain persistent settings, and even to install programs on the live CD using a number of complicated hacks. Installing programs on the live CD is complicated, because the entire */usr* and other important directories are read-only. To remedy this problem, Klaus has introduced the UnionFS system to Knoppix 3.8. (For more information on UnionFS, see *http://www.fsl.cs.sunysb.edu/project-unionfs.html*.)

The UnionFS system stacks your existing ramdisk on top of the read-only filesystem on the CD and keeps track of any files that have been modified on the fly. When you access a file in the filesystem that has been modified, UnionFS points you to the copy in ramdisk instead of the copy on the CD-ROM. This allows you to write to the complete filesystem as though Knoppix were installed to a hard drive.

With UnionFS, the live software installer is no longer necessary. You can now install all of the extra programs you want using standard Debian tools. For instance, to install the Enlightenment window manager, type:

```
$ sudo apt-get update
$ sudo apt-get install enlightenment
```

You can also use your favorite graphical installation tool under Debian with this method. All of the programs you install with this method are installed in their regular locations, and if you look at the */ramdisk* directory on the CD, you will see a mirror of the root directory structure with all of the files that you have changed.

UnionFS Persistence

The persistent home directory script has been updated to support UnionFS, so now you can maintain all changes to your filesystem from a persistent directory. The name of the script has changed, so to execute it from a terminal type:

```
knoppix@0[knoppix]$ knoppix-mkimage
```

To launch it graphically instead, click K → KNOPPIX → Config → "Create a persistent KNOPPIX disk image." Once the script launches, it behaves similarly to the old script and lets you choose which device to create the persistent file on and how large to make it. The script does provide some new features, however, such as the ability to automatically encrypt the home directory with AES256 encryption.

Once you boot, you no longer have to use the home cheat code, as Knoppix will automatically detect that you have a persistent home directory available. You can then choose which features to restore from that drive, or let Knoppix boot normally without loading any settings (which it will do automatically after a timeout).

Final Words

Knoppix is an incredibly flexible and useful tool, and this book covers only some of its more common uses. If you are interested in digging into the depths of Knoppix, or making your own highly customized CD based on it, I strongly recommend spending some time within the Knoppix community, particularly at *http://www.knoppix.net*. A number of skilled

Knoppix hackers browse the forums there. You can of course also read *Knoppix Hacks* (O'Reilly) for more detailed explanations of how to use Knoppix, along with many additional tips and tricks.

Acknowledgments

First of all, thanks to Joseph E. Esposito, who asked me if I would write a pocket-sized Knoppix book for him. Hope you enjoy it.

Thanks to my wife Joy, who kept me encouraged, motivated, and caffeinated throughout this process.

This book wouldn't be possible, of course, without Klaus Knopper's ingenuity. Knoppix seems to get better and better.

Last but not least, thanks to my editor, David Brickner, for all of his useful comments and corrections, and to Fabian Franz for his technical critique.

Index

We'd like to hear your suggestions for improving our indexes. Send email to
index@oreilly.com.

Related Titles Available from O'Reilly

Linux

Building Embedded Linux Systems

Building Secure Servers with Linux

The Complete FreeBSD, *4th Edition*

Even Grues Get Full

Exploring the JDS Linux Desktop

Extreme Programming Pocket Guide

Knoppix Hacks

Learning Red Hat Enterprise Linux and Fedora, *4th Edition*

Linux Cookbook

Linux Desktop Hacks

Linux Device Drivers, *3rd Edition*

Linux in a Nutshell, *4th Edition*

Linux iptables Pocket Reference

Linux Network Administrator's Guide, *3rd Edition*

Linux Pocket Guide

Linux Security Cookbook

Linux Server Hacks

Linux Unwired

Linux Web Server CD Bookshelf, *Version 2.0*

LPI Linux Certification in a Nutshell, *2nd Edition*

Managing RAID on Linux

OpenOffice.org Writer

Programming with Qt, *2nd Edition*

Root of all Evil

Running Linux, *4th Edition*

Samba Pocket Reference, *2nd Edition*

Test Driving Linux

Understanding the Linux Kernel, *2nd Edition*

Understanding Open Source & Free Software Licensing

User Friendly

Using Samba, *3rd Edition*

O'REILLY®

Our books are available at most retail and online bookstores.
To order direct: 1-800-998-9938 • *order@oreilly.com* • *www.oreilly.com*
Online editions of most O'Reilly titles are available at *safari.oreilly.com*

Keep in touch with O'Reilly

1. Download examples from our books

To find example files for a book, go to:
www.oreilly.com/catalog

select the book, and follow the "Examples" link.

2. Register your O'Reilly books

Register your book at *register.oreilly.com*

Why register your books? Once you've registered your O'Reilly books you can:

- Win O'Reilly books, T-shirts or discount coupons in our monthly drawing.
- Get special offers available only to registered O'Reilly customers.
- Get catalogs announcing new books (US and UK only).
- Get email notification of new editions of the O'Reilly books you own.

3. Join our email lists

Sign up to get topic-specific email announcements of new books and conferences, special offers, and O'Reilly Network technology newsletters at:
elists.oreilly.com

It's easy to customize your free elists subscription so you'll get exactly the O'Reilly news you want.

4. Get the latest news, tips, and tools
www.oreilly.com

- "Top 100 Sites on the Web"—PC Magazine
- CIO Magazine's Web Business 50 Awards

Our web site contains a library of comprehensive product information (including book excerpts and tables of contents), downloadable software, background articles, interviews with technology leaders, links to relevant sites, book cover art, and more.

5. Work for O'Reilly

Check out our web site for current employment opportunities:
jobs.oreilly.com

6. Contact us

O'Reilly & Associates
1005 Gravenstein Hwy North
Sebastopol, CA 95472 USA

TEL: 707-827-7000 or 800-998-9938
(6am to 5pm PST)

FAX: 707-829-0104

order@oreilly.com
For answers to problems regarding your order or our products.
To place a book order online, visit:
www.oreilly.com/order_new

catalog@oreilly.com
To request a copy of our latest catalog.

booktech@oreilly.com
For book content technical questions or corrections.

corporate@oreilly.com
For educational, library, government, and corporate sales.

proposals@oreilly.com
To submit new book proposals to our editors and product managers.

international@oreilly.com
For information about our international distributors or translation queries. For a list of our distributors outside of North America check out:
international.oreilly.com/distributors.html

adoption@oreilly.com
For information about academic use of O'Reilly books, visit:
academic.oreilly.com

O'REILLY®

Our books are available at most retail and online bookstores.
To order direct: 1-800-998-9938 • *order@oreilly.com* • *www.oreilly.com*
Online editions of most O'Reilly titles are available at *safari.oreilly.com*